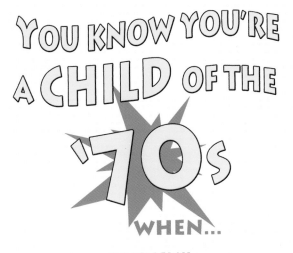

YOU KNOW YOU'RE A CHILD OF THE '70s WHEN...

MARK LEIGH
MIKE LEPINE

summersdale

YOU KNOW YOU'RE A CHILD OF THE '70s WHEN...

Text by Mike Lepine and Mark Leigh

Summersdale Publishers Ltd
46 West Street
Chichester
West Sussex
PO19 1RP
UK

www.summersdale.com

Printed and bound by Tien Wah Press, Singapore

ISBN: 1-84024-516-6
ISBN: 978-1-84024-516-5

Mike Lepine

Mike Lepine spent his formative teenage years in the 1970s and – despite the constantly changing fashions – couldn't fit in with any of them. He had no gender identity issues to work out with Glam, was far too reactionary for Prog, had absolutely no funky stuff whatsoever to strut during the 'difficult' Disco Years and thought that wearing a bin bag and gobbing at people was just another boring way of conforming. He did like those big Super Mousse chocolate bars, though...

Mark Leigh

Born in 1966, Mark Leigh grew up in the 1970s wanting to be the lead guitarist in Slade, the pilot of Skylab or the Fonz. He has vivid memories of a weird TV series called *H.R. Pufnstuf* but doesn't know if this really existed, or was just an hallucination from eating some out of date Spanish Gold sweet tobacco. Mark used to have fantasies about Olga Korbut, Ruth from Pan's People and Susan Stranks, and, if truth be known, still does.

THANK YOU TO

From Mike:
Philippa Hatton Lepine

From Mark:
Debbie, Polly and Barney.

You know you're a child of the '70s when...

You begged your
mum to knit you
a Clanger.

If asked to name a celebrity couple, you instantly reply 'Farrah Fawcett Majors and Lee Majors'.

You remember singles staying at number one for four weeks, not four days.

Close your eyes and
you can still taste
Mint Cracknell,
Amazin' Raisin
and Aztec bars.

Your adolescent fantasies involved Anthea Redfern, Marie Osmond and the blonde one from Abba (and sometimes all three).

You thought the three funniest men in the whole wide world were Tim Brooke-Taylor, Graeme Garden and Bill Oddie.

**You were scared
stiff of the Bermuda
Triangle.**

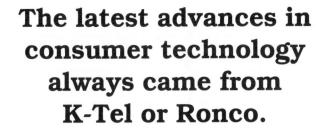

The latest advances in consumer technology always came from K-Tel or Ronco.

You used to bounce about on a spacehopper. Now you're starting to resemble one.

Your first taste of alcohol came from a lukewarm can of Top Deck Shandy.

Summer holidays were spent riding your Raleigh Chopper and imagining yourself as Barry Sheene or Evel Knievel.

You once thought
that the Fonz and
Alvin Stardust were
the hardest men
on the planet.

You wouldn't go out without first checking your mood ring and your biorhythms.

You spent your childhood kitted out in clothes from C&A – if you were that lucky.

You baffle your kids by doing Frank Spencer, Freddie 'Parrot Face' Davies and Charlie Williams impersonations.

Your idea of a supermodel was an Airfix 1:72 scale B-17 Flying Fortress.

You remember
when avocado was
the new black.

You grew up wanting to be Jason King, The Six Million Dollar Man or Charlie George – if you were a boy.

... or Daisy Duke,
Wonder Woman
or Kate Bush if
you were a girl.

You used to kid yourself that you looked like Bodie, and your best mate looked like Doyle.

You wore nail varnish, sequins and glitter – and didn't feel any less of a man for doing it.

Sophistication was pineapple and cheese on sticks and a glass of warm Cinzano.

You've never
forgiven your parents
for exposing you to
Roger Whittaker LPs.

Men's grooming products consisted of soap on a rope, a can of Cossack hairspray and a bottle of Hai Karate or Blue Stratos.

You find yourself muttering the catchphrases 'I 'ate you Butler', 'Nice one Cyril' and 'Uh-Oh Chongo'.

Your idea of an 'illegal download' was taping songs off the radio with a hand-held microphone.

You resented the
fact that everyone
was on strike except
schoolteachers.

You can still play *Stairway To Heaven* on your tennis racket.

You remember when chess matches made the sports pages of national newspapers.

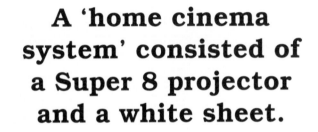

A 'home cinema system' consisted of a Super 8 projector and a white sheet.

The biggest decision you ever had to make was 'Donny Osmond or David Cassidy?'.

You were a member
of the Planet of the
Apes Fan Club *and*
the KISS Army.

You still occasionally crave a bottle of Cresta (*'It's frothy man!'*).

You spent a month
with your wrist in
plaster after an
horrific Klackers
accident.

You think that Dick Emery made a more convincing woman than David Walliams.

You put your atrocious spelling down to all those Slade song titles.

Having G-Plan furniture, wall-to-wall carpeting, a yucca plant and a through-lounge confirmed that your family were middle class.

Your dream car was a Ford Capri 2000 XL. That or a Lunar Roving vehicle.

You looked forward to watching *Ask The Family* and identifying the close-up black and white photo of a comb or a pencil sharpener.

You used to wear
tartan – and you
aren't remotely
Scottish.

You once started each day with a bowl of Puffa Puffa Rice or Golden Nuggets.

You'd spend hours
in Miss Selfridge
discussing the
various merits of
baggies, parallels,
bell-bottoms
or flares.

You can remember when there were 'cod wars' and your parents reassured you that Iceland would never resort to 'the nuclear option'.

All your pocket money was spent on Pink Panther Bars, Bazooka Joe's and *Countdown* comics.

You not only know what carbon paper is, but you used it regularly in your first office job.

You could once enthral 30 classmates just by showing off your new blakeys.

Marc Bolan and his feather boa got you all confused about your sexuality...
at just the wrong time of life.

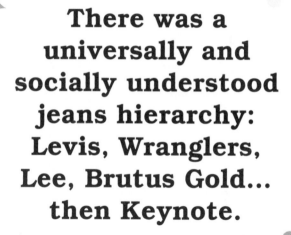

There was a universally and socially understood jeans hierarchy: Levis, Wranglers, Lee, Brutus Gold... then Keynote.

You can't quite convey to your children just how good a Lord Toffingham ice lolly tasted...

You managed to sneak in, underaged, to see *The Exorcist* – and then spent many sleepless nights wishing you hadn't.

You and your friends had a gang based around *The Tomorrow People*.

40 was the average age of children's TV presenters – not their IQ.

Each time you visit the cinema you still secretly crave a carton of Kia-Ora and a box of Toffets.

You'll never forget the day the Phantom Flan-Flinger attacked the St Winifred's School Choir on *Tiswas*.

You can remember
a time when
dark brown and
cheesecloth
weren't considered
fashion crimes.

TV ad breaks featured useful public information films warning you about the perils of playing near railway lines and accepting lifts from strangers.

You think Queen's 'Bohemian Rhapsody' is the greatest pop video ever made.

You attribute
your short-term
memory loss to all
the chemicals in
the Parma Violets
you scoffed down
back then.

You and your mates all had a favourite one from *Charlie's Angels* and you'd spend hours arguing who was the tastiest.

You went to a
football match
specifically to kick
someone's head in.

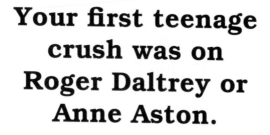

Your first teenage
crush was on
Roger Daltrey or
Anne Aston.

Your child's weekly pocket money is more than you earned when you first started work.

You wished you
could be adopted by
the Partridge Family.

Staying in a half-built hotel in Magaluf or Benidorm was considered an exotic holiday.

The most powerful
computer in your
home was an
Atari 2600 with
128 colours.

You really believed that Gary Numan was radical, avant-garde and rebellious – and not a pasty-faced arse.

You once thought the sight of Terry Scott dressed as a schoolboy was funny (and not deeply disturbing).

You can sing all
the words to 'The
Lumberjack Song'
from beginning
to end.

All the clothes you wore back then (and your haircuts) can now be found on humorous birthday cards.

You could always count on your best friend's mum to give you a glass of warm, semi-flat Tizer.

You remember when the Americans elected a peanut farmer as president... and thinking they couldn't get any more ludicrous than that.

You were genuinely shocked when you found out where pop group 10CC got their name from.

You thought you laughed out loud at *The Two Ronnies*. Now, seeing re-runs of the show, you know you must have been mistaken.

You sometimes get the urge to put your fingers in your belt loops and do the 'Tiger Feet' dance.

A rite of passage was heralded by changing from *Beezer* and *The Dandy* to *Whizzer and Chips* and *Cor!!*

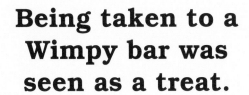

Being taken to a
Wimpy bar was
seen as a treat.

You used to have a cassette of *Derek and Clive* that you kept hidden from your mum.

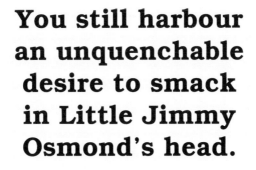

You still harbour
an unquenchable
desire to smack
in Little Jimmy
Osmond's head.

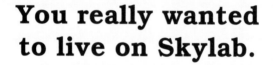

You really wanted
to live on Skylab.

You tell anyone who'll listen that Karl Douglas could kick Jackie Chan or Jet Li's butt.

You find yourself scouring eBay for that elusive 1970s World Cup Squad coin collection or the *Sun*'s football stamp album.

You're hugely disappointed because Ted Heath is dead now – and your suspicions may never be confirmed.

You think radio peaked with *The Kenny Everett Show* and the genius that was Captain Kremmen.

You wanted your dad to paint a white stripe down the side of his Mk III Cortina so you could pretend you and he were Starsky and Hutch.

The biggest, most bad-ass rappers you'd ever seen were the Sugarhill Gang.

You never could quite work up the nerve to push a safety pin through your nose, but you knew you were a punk at heart.

You're still trying
to figure out what
'Can the Can'
was all about.

Somewhere, in a safely guarded keepsake box, is your 'Rock Against Racism' badge.

You know that
Tavares is NOT a
tropical disease.

You can't believe you were ever engrossed in a soap about a North Sea ferry starring Kate O'Mara.

All the great songs
of your childhood
are readily available
on free CDs with the
weekend newspapers.